Top 40 Asia Recipes

The Most Authentic Asian Soup Cookbook

BY

Daniel Humphreys

Copyright 2019 Daniel Humphreys

License Notes

No part of this Book can be reproduced in any form or by any means including print, electronic, scanning or photocopying unless prior permission is granted by the author.

All ideas, suggestions and guidelines mentioned here are written for informative purposes. While the author has taken every possible step to ensure accuracy, all readers are advised to follow information at their own risk. The author cannot be held responsible for personal and/or commercial damages in case of misinterpreting and misunderstanding any part of this Book

Table of Contents

Introduction 6

   Hot Sour Soup 8

   Veggie Noodle Soup 11

   Japanese Onion Soup 14

   Chili Laksa Soup 17

   Egg Drop Soup 20

   Curried Carrot Soup 22

   Curried Pork-Stuffed Wonton Soup 25

   Coconut Chicken Soup 28

   Vegan Pho 31

   Powerful Miso Soup 34

   Tom Yum Soup 37

   Spicy Beef Soup 40

   Chicken Sotanghon Soup 43

   Garlicky Bok Choy and Chicken Soup 46

   Spicy and Gingery Scallion Soup 49

Chinese Cabbage and Pork Meatball Soup 52

Easy Pork and Daikon Soup 55

Quick Mushroom Ramen Soup 57

Mushroom and Broccoli Asian Soup 59

Tofu Cilantro Soup 62

Kombu, Cabbage, and Chicken Japanese Soup 64

Hot and Sour Shrimp Soup 67

Lotus Root and Pork Soup 69

Coconut and Kaffir Tomato Soup 71

Bok Choy and Poached Egg Udon Soup 74

Clam Miso Soup 77

Winter Melon Soup 79

Hibachi Soup 81

Quick Kimchi Ramen Soup 83

Sriracha Zucchini Soup 86

Chinese Seaweed and Pork Soup 88

Japanese Rice Soup 91

Korean Soybean Soup 94

Kabocha Squash Soup 96

Instant Short Rib Soup 99

Coconut and Lentil Soup 101

Mason Jar Pho Soup 104

Thai Soup with Pumpkin and Coconut 106

Gingery and Garlicky Turmeric and Tofu Soup 109

Vietnamese Sour Fish Soup 112

Conclusion 115

Author's Afterthoughts 116

About the Author 117

Introduction

Has your imagination taken a break? Struggling to find the best way to put the soy sauce, miso paste, and tofu to use? Don't worry, we are here to offer you a helping hand.

This cookbook will not only enrich your recipe folder by 40 superfood Asian soups that will nourish you from the inside out, but it will also turn you into a master of the Asian cuisine. Delightful and rich in the most amazing Asian flavors, the soups found in this book are both incredibly healthy and mind-blowingly delicious.

Vegetarian, vegan, or a meat lover, these recipes will definitely please the tummies of everyone who tries them.

So, grab your pot, jump to the first recipe, and start cooking. I dare you to pick a favorite soup.

Hot Sour Soup

Rich in amazing flavors, super tasty, easy to make, and ready in just 15 minutes, this hot and sour soup will nourish your bellies in a jiffy. This is a vegetarian recipe, but you can substitute the tofu with pork if you want to.

Serves: 6-8

Ready In: 15 minutes

Ingredients:

- ¼ cup Soy Sauce
- ¼ cup Cornstarch
- ¼ cup Rice Wine Vinegar
- 8 cups Veggie Stock
- 2 tsp ground Ginger
- 8 ounces Shitake Mushrooms, sliced
- 4 Green Onions, sliced
- 1 tsp Chili Garlic Sauce
- 2 Eggs, whisked
- 1 tsp Sesame Oil

Preparation:

Set aside about ½ cup of the stock and place the rest of it in a large pot.

Stir in the rice wine vinegar, soy sauce, mushrooms, chili garlic sauce, and ginger.

Bring to a simmer over medium heat.

Meanwhile, whisk together the cornstarch and remaining stock.

Stir into the soup and cook until thickened.

Drizzle the eggs over, and stir in a circular motion, to make egg ribbons.

Stir in the remaining ingredients.

Serve immediately and enjoy.

Veggie Noodle Soup

Packed with healthy and nutritious veggies, and rich in protein thanks to the yummy tofu, this Asian noodle soup with a bunch of veggies is the best way to up your vitamin and mineral intake.

Serves: 6-8

Ready In: 15 minutes

Ingredients:

- 8 cups Water
- 1 package Shirataki Noodles
- ½ tsp ground Ginger
- 2 tbsp. Soy Sauce
- 2 tbsp. Veggie Bouillon
- 1 tsp Sriracha
- 1 bundle of Bok Choy, diced
- 1 package Tofu, cubed
- ½ Yellow Onion, sliced
- 2 cups Mushroom Slices
- 1 tbsp. Miso
- 4 Garlic Cloves, minced

Preparation:

Combine the water, ginger, miso, bouillon, sriracha, and soy sauce, in a large pot over medium heat. Bring to a boil.

Stir in the veggies and cook for 5 minutes.

Stir in the noodles and tofu and cook for 3 more minutes.

Serve immediately topped with your favorite toppings.

Enjoy!

Japanese Onion Soup

Clear Japanese soup with onions, scallions, mushrooms, celery, and carrots, for a nourishing and mood uplifting lunch. Serve topped with some green onions and enjoy.

Serves: 4

Ready In: 40 minutes

Ingredients:

- 6 cups Veggie Broth
- 2 Onions, diced
- 7 Handfuls of Sliced Scallions
- 6 Handfuls of sliced Button Mushrooms
- 2 Celery Stalks, diced
- 2 Garlic Cloves, minced
- 2 Carrots, diced
- 1 tbsp. Soy Sauce
- 1 tsp Sriracha
- Salt and Pepper, to taste

Preparation:

Grease a large pot with some cooking spray.

Then add the onions and sauté until soft.

Add broth, carrots, garlic, and celery, and bring to a boil.

Stir in the soy sauce and sriracha, and cook for 25 minutes.

Stir in the mushrooms and scallions and cook for additional 5 minutes.

Season with salt and pepper, to taste.

Serve immediately and enjoy.

Chili Laksa Soup

This Malaysian classic will warm your tummies like nothing else. If you are not a big chili lover, I suggest you bring the chilliness in this recipe down a notch. Serve with rice noodles if preferred.

Serves: 6

Ready In: 15 minutes

Ingredients:

Laksa Paste:

- 6 dried Red Chilies, soaked in boiling water for 10 minutes
- 6 Cashews
- Juice and Zest of 1 Lime
- 1 Thai Red Chili, seeded
- 1 tbsp. Chili Paste
- 2 Shallots, chopped
- 5 Garlic Cloves
- 3-inch piece of Ginger
- 2 tbsp. Olive Oil

Soup:

- 1 cup Coconut Soup
- 2 tsp Sugar
- 2 cups Veggie Stock
- 1 Zucchini, sliced
- 2 tbsp. Lime Juice
- ¼ pound Tofu, sliced
- ½ tsp Salt

Preparation:

Place all of the laksa paste ingredients in your food processor.

Pulse until smooth.

Heat half of the laksa paste in a pot over medium heat.

Sauté for 1 minutes then add the zucchini and cook for 2 minutes.

Stir in the remaining ingredients.

Bring the soup to a boil and cook for 2 minutes.

Serve immediately and enjoy.

Egg Drop Soup

A yummy Asian egg drop soup for a satisfying lunch. This recipe uses enoki mushrooms, but you can easily substitute them with cremini or button mushrooms and get the same luxurious taste.

Serves: 4

Ready In: 20 minutes

Ingredients:

- 1 tbsp. Soy Sauce
- 1 tbsp. Cornstarch
- 3 Eggs, beaten
- ¼ tsp White Pepper
- ¾ cup sliced Enoki Mushrooms
- ½ tsp grated Ginger
- 4 cups Chicken Stock

Preparation:

Whisk together ½ cup of the stock with the cornstarch.

Combine the remaining ingredients, except the eggs, in a large pot.

Bring to a boil over medium heat.

Stir in the cornstarch mixture.

Reduce the heat and simmer until thickened.

Drizzle the eggs over, and stir in a circular motion to make egg ribbons.

Serve immediately and enjoy.

Curried Carrot Soup

Creamy, delicious, spicy, and sweet, this classic Thai soup is low in calories but rich in feel-good flavor. And the best part? It is 100 percent vegan and guilt-free, so don't worry about the refills.

Serves: 4

Ready In: 30 minutes

Ingredients:

- 1 tbsp. Brown Sugar
- 2 Garlic Cloves, chopped
- 2 tbsp. Curry Paste
- 4 cups Veggie Broth
- 2 tsp Curry Powder
- ¼ cup Peanut Butter
- 1 tbsp. Coconut Oil
- 1 tbsp. Ginger Paste
- 1 cup chopped Onions
- 1 ¼ pounds Carrots, sliced

Preparation:

Melt the coconut oil in a large pot over medium heat.

Add garlic and onion and cook for 3 minutes.

Add the ginger paste and cook for 30 seconds.

Stir in the curry powder, curry paste, carrots, sugar, and peanut butter.

Pour the broth over and bring to a boil.

Reduce the heat and simmer for 35 minutes.

Blend the soup with a blender if you want to.

Serve immediately and enjoy.

Curried Pork-Stuffed Wonton Soup

Ground pork, wonton wrappers, curry paste, and coconut milk play the main roles in this amazingly pleasing Asian soup recipe. Serve topped with some chopped peanuts and enjoy the rich taste.

Serves: 6-8

Ready In: 45 minutes

Ingredients:

Wontons:

- ¼ pound ground Pork
- 20 Wonton Wrappers
- 2 tsp Soy Sauce
- 2 Green Onions, sliced
- ½ tsp Sesame Oil
- 2 tbsp. minced Carrot
- 2 tbsp. minced Onions

Broth:

- 1 tbsp. Coconut Oil
- 4 cups Chicken Stock
- ½ cup chopped Onions
- 2 ½ tbsp. Brown Sugar
- 2 Garlic Cloves, minced
- 4 ½ tbsp. Red Curry Paste
- 2 ½ tbsp. Peanut Butter
- 1 ½ tsp Salt
- ½ tsp grated Ginger
- 14 ounces Coconut Milk

Preparation:

In a bowl, combine all of the wonton ingredients, except the wonton wrappers.

Fill each wonton wrapper with about a teaspoon of the pork filling.

Brush the edges with water, fold, bring the edges together, and seal.

Melt the coconut oil in a large pot.

Stir in the garlic and onion. Sauté for 2 minutes.

Add the curry and sauté for another minute.

Stir in the remaining ingredients and bring the soup to a boil.

Reduce the heat and simmer for 10 minutes.

Add the wontons and cook for 6 minutes.

Serve immediately and enjoy.

Coconut Chicken Soup

Originally called Tom Kha Gai, this Thai soup with coconut milk, chicken, mushrooms, and lemongrass, is packed with the most authentic Asian flavors that you are looking for in an Asian soup bowl.

Serves: 6-8

Ready In: 25 minutes

Ingredients:

- 2 cups shredded Chicken
- 2 cans Coconut Milk
- 2 Stalks Lemongrass, cut into 1-inch pieces
- 6 cups Chicken Broth
- ¼ cup Lime Juice
- 2 tbsp. Fish Sauce
- 2 tsp Coconut Sugar
- 8 ounces Oyster Mushrooms, sliced
- 4 Green Onions, sliced
- 2 tbsp. grated Ginger

Preparation:

Add the lemongrass, broth, lime juice, ginger and the white parts of the green onions to a large pot.

Place over high heat and bring to a boil.

Reduce to medium and cook for 10 minutes.

Strain the broth and return it back to the pot.

Stir in the mushrooms, coconut milk, chicken, sugar, and fish sauce.

Cook for 3 minutes.

Serve immediately topped with the green parts of the green onions.

Enjoy!

Vegan Pho

Simple ingredients and even simpler cooking steps for a rich and very satisfying pho. Made in 30 minutes, this is the most flavorful pho you will ever try.

Serves: 2-4

Ready In: 30 minutes

Ingredients:

- 2 Green Onions, sliced
- 2 Baby Bok Choy, quartered
- 2 Star Anise
- 2 Carrots, julienned
- 1 Onion, diced
- 2 Whole Cloves
- 4 cups Veggie Broth
- 2 Garlic Cloves, minced
- 4 ounces Shitake Mushrooms, sliced
- 1 tbsp. Soy Sauce
- 1 Cinnamon Stick

Preparation:

Place the cinnamon stick, cloves, and anise, in a pot over medium heat.

Roast for 30 seconds.

Stir in the broth, garlic, ginger, and onions.

Cover the pot and bring the soup to a boil.

Simmer for 15 minutes.

Strain the broth and return it back to the pot.

Stir in the remaining ingredients except the bok choy and cook for 10 minutes

Add the bok choy and cook for 3 more minutes.

Serve with your favorite toppings and enjoy.

Powerful Miso Soup

Miso, tofu, mushrooms, kombu, spinach, and scallions give this soup a powerful kick rich in essential vitamins and nutrients that will improve your immune system and warm your belly at the same time.

Serves: 6-8

Ready In: 1 hour and 35 minutes

Ingredients:

- 12 ounces Tofu, cubed
- 2 cups Baby Spinach
- 6 dried Shitake Mushrooms
- 2 pieces of Kombu
- 5 tbsp. Miso Paste
- 1 cup Bonito Flakes
- 2 Scallions, chopped
- 12 ounces Water

Preparation:

Rinse the kombu and mushrooms and place them in a large pot along with the 12 cups of water.

Let soak for about an hour.

Place the pot over medium heat and discard the kombu. Bring to a boil.

Add the bonito flakes and simmer for 20 minutes.

Strain the soup, whisk in the miso, and cook for 20 minutes.

Stir in spinach, tofu, and scallions.

Cook for about 5 minutes.

Serve immediately and enjoy.

Tom Yum Soup

If you love shrimp and the rich flavors of the Asian cuisine, then you will definitely be excited about the tom yum soup. This recipe is for the most authentic version of this classic Thai soup.

Serves: 4

Ready In: 25 minutes

Ingredients:

- 1 Garlic Clove, minced
- 8 cups Chicken Broth
- 3 tbsp. Tom Yum Paste
- 1 pound Rice Noodles, cooked
- ¼ cup minced Lemongrass
- 3 tbsp. Lime Juice
- 3 Lime Leaves
- 20 Shrimp, peeled and deveined
- 3 tbsp. Fish Sauce
- 1 cup of Coconut Milk

Preparation:

Combine the broth, tom yum paste, lemongrass, lime leaves, and garlic, in a large pot.

Bring to a boil over medium heat, and then simmer for 10 minutes.

Stir in the coconut milk, lime juice, and fish sauce, and cook for 3 minutes.

Add the shrimp and cook for another 3 minutes.

Stir in the noodles.

Serve immediately and enjoy!

Spicy Beef Soup

Spicy, delicious, rich in flavor, and really simple to make, this beef noodle soup will satisfy even those that don't like soup. Serve for lunch and see why homemade is always better.

Serves: 8

Ready In: 3 hours and 40 minutes

Ingredients:

- 5 Star Anise
- 16 cups Water
- 3 pounds Beef Chuck
- 3 tbsp. Oil
- 6 Ginger Sliced
- ¼ cup Shaoxing Wine
- 1 Onion, chopped
- 1 Tomato, chopped
- 4 Bay Leaves
- 1 tbsp. Sichuan Peppercorns
- ¼ cup spicy Bean Paste
- 1 tbsp. Sugar
- 1 piece of Tangerine Peel
- ½ cup Soy Sauce

Preparation:

Place the water in one large pot. Stir in the beef, wine, scallions, and ginger.

Bring to a boil over medium heat and let simmer for 10 minutes. Set aside.

In another pot, heat the oil over medium heat.

Add onion, garlic, peppercorn, bay leaves, and star anise.

Cook for 5 minutes then stir in the bean paste.

Add tomatoes and cook for 2 minutes.

Stir in the sugar and soy sauce and set aside,

Transfer the beef, ginger, scallions, and ginger form the first pot t the second pot.

Strain the broth and transfer it to the second pot.

Add the tangerine peel and bring the mixture to a boil.

Lower the heat and simmer for 90 minutes.

Then turn off the heat and let the soup sit for one hour.

Discard the peel.

Just before serving, bring the soup to a boil once again.

Serve and enjoy.

Chicken Sotanghon Soup

Famous in the Philippines, this chicken sotanghon soup satisfies everyone who tries it. Cabbage, eggs, and sotanghon noodles accompany the chicken and make one nourishing soup.

Serves: 6

Ready In: 35 minutes

Ingredients:

- 6 Hardboiled Eggs
- 1 pound Chicken Breast
- 8 cups Water
- 1 Onion, chopped
- 1 Chicken Broth Cube
- 2 cups Cabbage strips
- 2 tbsp. Oil
- ½ cup chopped Green Onion
- 6 Garlic Cloves, minced
- 3 tbsp. Fish Sauce
- 1 Carrot, grated
- 1 tsp Achuete Powder
- 4 ounces Sotanghon Noodles

Preparation:

Pour the water in a large pot and cook the chicken for about 15 minutes, or until no longer pink. Transfer to a plate and slice.

In a large pot, heat the oil over medium heat.

Set 1 tbsp. of the garlic aside. Add the onions and rest of the garlic to the pot, and cook for 3 minutes.

Stir in the chicken broth (the liquid where you cooked the chicken) and broth cube.

Take ½ cup of the broth and combine it with the achuete powder. Stir this mixture into the soup.

Add noodles, chicken, carrots, cabbage, and cook for 2 minutes.

Serve topped with a halved egg and enjoy!

Garlicky Bok Choy and Chicken Soup

If you are looking for something that will help you fight the flu, you will not find a better weapon than this vitamin-packed and nourishing soup. Make a large batch and drink throughout the day. So yummy!

Serves: 4

Ready In: 30 minutes

Ingredients:

- 1 tsp Turmeric Powder
- ½ tsp Cayenne Pepper
- 6 Garlic Cloves, minced
- 1 tbsp. Soy Sauce
- 1 tbsp. Olive Oil
- 1 cup chopped Kale
- 1 cup chopped Bok Choy
- 10 Mushrooms, sliced
- 3 Chicken Breasts, diced
- 5 cups Chicken Stock
- 3 cups Water
- 1 Onion, chopped

Preparation:

Heat the oil in a large pot over medium heat.

Add onions and cook for 3 minutes.

Add garlic and cook for another minute.

Add chicken and cook until no longer pink.

Pour the water and broth over.

Stir in the spices and bring to a boil.

Cook on low for 15 minutes.

Add mushrooms, kale, and bok choy, and cook for 5 more minutes.

Serve and enjoy!

Spicy and Gingery Scallion Soup

Ginger is one of the 'absolute musts' in the Asian soups, and this one is packed with it. Simple ingredients create one unforgettable taste and very pleasant flavor that will satisfy everyone.

Serves: 4

Ready In: 20 minutes

Ingredients:

- 1 Cinnamon Stick
- 2 cups Water
- 4 cups Veggie Broth
- 1 tsp Sesame Oil
- 2 tbsp. Olive Oil
- 2 Garlic Cloves, minced
- 3 tbsp. Lime Juice
- 4 Rice Noodles, cooked
- 3 tbsp. Soy Sauce
- 2 tbsp. minced Ginger
- 2 cups sliced Mushrooms
- 1 bunch Scallions, sliced

Preparation:

Heat the olive oil in a large pot over medium heat.

Add the scallion and ginger and cook for about 2 minutes.

Stir in the mushrooms, sriracha, and soy sauce, and cook for more 2 minutes.

Stir in the broth, water and add the cinnamon stick. Bring to a boil and let simmer for 5 minutes.

Discard the cinnamon and stir in the noodles and sesame oil.

Serve and enjoy!

Chinese Cabbage and Pork Meatball Soup

Looking for an authentic Chinese soup t warm you up during the cold winter days? You will not find a better recipe than this one. Rich and delightful, the flavors that are combined in a pot of this soup will bring a smile to your face.

Serves: 8

Ready In: 60 minutes

Ingredients:

Meatballs:

- 1 ½ tbsp. Cornstarch
- ¼ cup minced Shrimp
- ½ pound ground Pork
- 1 tsp Soy Sauce
- ½ tsp salt
- ¼ cup diced Water Chestnuts
- ½ tsp Sugar

Soup:

- 2 tsp Salt
- 2 tsp Soy Sauce
- 10 cups Chicken Stock
- 1 Carrot, diced
- ½ head Napa Cabbage chopped
- 2 tsp Sesame Seeds

Preparation:

Combine all of the meatball ingredients in a bowl and let marinate for 15 minutes.

Place the stock in a pot and then bring it to a boil.

Add carrot and cabbage and cook for 30 minutes.

Roll the pork mixture into meatballs.

Drop the meatballs into the soup. Cook for about 3 minutes.

Stir in the remaining ingredients.

Serve and enjoy!

Easy Pork and Daikon Soup

Another Chinese classic that will blow your mind with its incredibly delicious taste. Delicate in flavor with a hint of saltiness, this soup will be your ultimate lunch.

Serves: 6-8

Ready In: 2 hours and 15 minutes

Ingredients:

- 4 dried Scallops
- 1 pound Pork, cut into pieces
- 10 ounces Daikon, peeled and chopped
- ½ tsp Salt
- 10 cups Veggie Broth or Water

Preparation:

Place the broth or water in a large pot.

Stir in the remaining ingredients.

Bring to a boil over the medium heat.

Lower the heat to low and let it simmer for 2 hours.

Serve and enjoy!

Quick Mushroom Ramen Soup

Ready in just 15 minutes, this easy to make Asian soup with oyster mushrooms, bok choy, eggs, and egg noodles, is packed with the most amazing flavors.

Serves: 4

Ready In: 15 minutes

Ingredients:

- 4 Eggs
- 4 Baby Bok Choy, halved
- 7 ½ cups Vegetable Broth
- 2 tbsp. Soy Sauce

- 6 ½ ounces Egg Noodles
- 7 ounces Oyster Mushrooms
- 4 Spring Onions, sliced

Preparation:

Fill a saucepan with water, bring it to a boil, and cook the eggs for 6 minutes.

Let cool before cutting in half.

Meanwhile, place the stock in a large pot, and bring it to a boil over the medium heat.

Add the mushrooms, and allow to simmer on low for 3 minutes.

Add noodles, increase the heat to medium, and cook for 3 minutes.

Stir in the remaining ingredients.

Cook for 2 minutes.

Serve with halved eggs.

Enjoy!

Mushroom and Broccoli Asian Soup

Veggie packed Asian soup that is so comforting that will definitely keep you coming back for refills. Healthy, vegan, and gluten-free, this is the best immune booster.7

Serves: 8

Ready In: 20 minutes

Ingredients:

- 8 cups Veggie Broth
- 1 Onion, diced
- 2 tbsp. Olive Oil
- 2 Bay Leaves
- 1 tsp Sugar
- 1 tbsp. Rice Vinegar
- 1 cups Broccoli Florets
- 12 ounces Mushrooms, sliced
- 1 tbsp. Apple Cider Vinegar
- 1 tsp Thyme
- 1 tsp black Pepper
- 3 Garlic Cloves, minced
- 1 tsp grated Ginger
- 1 tbsp. Soy Sauce

Preparation:

Heat the oil in a large pot and sauté the onions for 3 minutes.

Add garlic and ginger and cook for 30 seconds.

Stir in the remaining ingredients.

Bring the soup to a boil.

Simmer on low for 15 minutes.

Serve and enjoy!

Tofu Cilantro Soup

Tofu and cilantro are the stars of this recipe and give this Asian soup a fresh taste that will nourish you from the inside out. Serve with noodles if you want to, for a more filling meal.

Serves: 2

Ready In: 15 minutes

Ingredients:

- ½ tsp Lemon Juice
- 2 cups Veggie Broth
- ¼ tsp Black Pepper
- 1 tsp Olive Oil
- ¼ cup Broccoli Florets
- ¼ cup chopped Carrots
- ½ cup chopped Cilantro
- 1 tbsp. Soy Sauce
- 1 cup chopped Tofu

Preparation:

Heat the oil along with the cilantro in a pot.

Cook for 30 seconds before adding the broccoli and carrots.

After 30 seconds, stir in the tofu and cook for 1 minute.

Stir in the remaining ingredients.

Bring to a boil, and cook over medium heat for 6 minutes.

Serve and enjoy!

Kombu, Cabbage, and Chicken Japanese Soup

Clear, elegant, and super delicious, this Japanese soup will warm you up even on the coldest days. Add a half of a tablespoon in it for a tangier taste, if desired.

Serves: 4

Ready In: 25 minutes

Ingredients:

- 1 piece of Kombu
- 12 ounces Chicken Breasts, cooked and shredded
- 1 Leek, sliced
- ½ Cabbage Head, chopped
- 1 Carrot, grated
- 1 cups Chicken Broth
- 1 cup chopped Kale
- 1 cup sliced Mushrooms
- 1 tbsp. Soy Sauce
- 1 tbsp. Coconut Oil
- 1 tsp minced Garlic
- 1 tsp minced Ginger

Preparation:

Melt the coconut oil in a pot over the medium heat.

Add leeks and cook for 3 minutes.

Add garlic and ginger and cook for one more minute.

Add kombu, cabbage, and stock. Bring to a boil.

Cover and cook for 10 minutes.

Discard the kombu.

Add the remaining ingredients and cook for 4 more minutes.

Serve and enjoy!

Hot and Sour Shrimp Soup

A different take of the classic tom yum soup that will leave you breathless with its rich flavor and irresistible taste. Serve with some crusty bread. I guarantee you will be licking your bowl in no time.

Serves: 4

Ready In: 20 minutes

Ingredients:

- 2 cups Water
- 2 cups Chicken Broth
- 4 Lime Leaves
- 2 Chilies, deseeded and sliced
- 1 tsp Brown Sugar
- 2 tbsp. Lime Juice
- 4 ounces Shitake Mushrooms, sliced
- 2 Shallots, sliced
- 2 Lemongrass Stalks, sliced
- 1 tbsp. Fish Sauce
- 1 pound Shrimp, peeled and deveined

Preparation:

Combine the broth, lemongrass, shallots, lime leaves, water, mushrooms, and chili, in a pot over medium heat.

Bring to a boil and add the shrimp.

Cook for 3 minutes.

Stir in the remaining ingredient and cook for 1 minute.

Serve and enjoy!

Lotus Root and Pork Soup

Although lotus rot is definitely the star of this recipe, the pork, peanuts, and dates are in charge of complementing the taste and give this soup incredible flavor that is simply hard to resist.

Serves: 4

Ready In: 2 hours and 15 minutes

Ingredients:

- 1 long Lotus Root (about 1 pound), sliced
- 1 Carrot, diced
- 1 pound Pork Ribs, chopped
- 4 ounces Peanuts, soaked in boiling water for 30 minutes
- 8 dried Red Dates
- 4 dried Scallops, soaked in hot water for 10 minutes
- Water, as needed

Preparation:

Place all of the ingredients in a large pot.

Pour enough water to submerge them by 2 inches.

Bring the mixture to a boil over medium heat.

Reduce to low and cook for almost 2 hours.

Serve and enjoy!

Coconut and Kaffir Tomato Soup

If you love eating tomato soup but are boring of the classic Pomodoro version, then I highly suggest you give this recipe a try. A Thai tomato soup with coconut milk, kaffir lime leaves and lemongrass.

Serves: 3

Ready In: 40 minutes

Ingredients:

- 1 cup Basil Leaves
- ¼ cup Coconut Milk
- 3 Garlic Cloves, minced
- 1 pint Cherry Tomatoes, halved
- 1 tbsp. Olive Oil
- 1 inch Lemongrass Stalk, sliced
- 1 Onion, diced
- 1 ½ cups Vegetable Broth
- 28 ounces canned ground Tomatoes

Preparation:

Preheat your oven to 400 degrees F.

Arrange the tomatoes with the cut side down on a greased baking tray.

Bake for 20 minutes.

Heat the olive oil in a large pot.

Add onions and cook for 3 minutes.

Add garlic and cook for 30 seconds.

Add the ground tomatoes, lime leaves, broth, and lemongrass.

Stir and simmer for 20 minutes.

Stir in basil and coconut milk.

Serve and enjoy!

Bok Choy and Poached Egg Udon Soup

Flavored with cinnamon, this Asian soup with udon noodles, poached eggs, and bok choy is a real powerhouse that will nourish your senses.

Serves:

Ready In: 20 minutes

Ingredients:

- 2 cups Veggie Broth
- 3 tbsp. Soy Sauce
- 4 large Bok Choy Leaves, chopped
- 2 Spring Onions, sliced
- 2 Eggs
- 7 ounces Udon Noodles
- 1 Cinnamon Stick
- 2 Whole Star Anise

Preparation:

Bring the broth to a boil in a saucepan.

Add cinnamon and star anise and cook for 5 minutes.

Remove the spices from the pan.

Crack one egg in a cup and slip it into the soup. Repeat with the other egg.

Cook for 2 minutes.

Add the bok choy, noodles, and soy sauce.

Cook for 2 minutes.

Serve and enjoy!

Clam Miso Soup

Originally called Asari Miso Soup, this Asian soup with mushrooms, tofu, miso paste, and clams, make a great lunch that will pack you with feel-good vibes. This recipe uses Buna Shimeiji mushrooms, but you can use any type you want.

Serves: 3

Ready In: 15 minutes

Ingredients:

- 2 tbsp. Miso Paste
- 3 cups Water
- ½ Tofu Block, cubed
- ½ pound Clams
- 2 ounces Buna Shimeiji Mushrooms, sliced

Preparation:

Place the water in a saucepan and bring it to a boil.

Stir in the clams, tofu, and mushrooms. Cook for 3 minutes.

Turn off the heat and stir in the miso paste.

Serve immediately and enjoy!

Winter Melon Soup

Packed with some impressive health properties, the white melon makes this soup a real powerhouse that your immune system will be extremely grateful for. Use tofu instead of the pork ribs for a vegetarian version.

Serves: 8

Ready In: 1 hour

Ingredients:

- 1 pound Pork Ribs
- 8 cups Water
- 1 tbsp. Goji Berries
- 8 Red Dates
- ½ Winter Melon, chopped
- 1 tsp Salt

Preparation:

Combine the pork, water, red dates, and winter melon, in a large pot.

Bring to a boil, reduce to a simmer, and cook for 45-60 minutes.

Stir in the remaining ingredients.

Bring the soup back to a boil, and remove from heat.

Serve immediately and enjoy!

Hibachi Soup

This gingery and vitamin-packed veggie Asian soup will prove you how delicious can a combination of simple ingredients really be. Top with a hardboiled or poached egg for a more filling meal.

Serves: 6

Ready In: 20 minutes

Ingredients:

- 1 cup sliced Mushrooms
- 3 tbsp. Beef Bouillon Granules
- 2 tbsp. Chicken Bouillon Granules
- 2 Carrots, chopped
- ½ Celery Stalk, chopped
- 2 tbsp. chopped Ginger
- 3 Garlic Cloves, minced
- 8 cups Water
- 1 Onion, chopped
- 2 tsp Soy Sauce

Preparation:

Combine all of the ingredients in a large pot.

Bring it to a boil over medium heat.

Reduce to a simmer and cook for 15 minutes.

Serve immediately.

Enjoy!

Quick Kimchi Ramen Soup

Kimchi cabbage and kimchi juice give this soup a very specific flavor that your guests will absolutely love. This recipe uses instant noodles but, if you want to, you can use spiralized veggies instead.

Serves: 2

Ready In: 15 minutes

Ingredients:

- 1 package Instant Noodles
- 5 Shitake Mushrooms, sliced
- 1 tbsp. Oil
- ¼ tsp Sugar
- ½ cup chopped Kimchi Cabbage
- ¼ cup Kimchi Juice
- 1 tsp Sesame Oil
- 1 Scallion, julienned
- 2 tsp Korean Red Pepper Powder

Preparation:

Heat the oil in a saucepan.

Add the mushrooms and cook for 3 minutes.

Add the kimchi and cook for another 2 minutes.

Stir in the stock, sugar, red pepper, sesame oil, and kimchi juice.

Bring the mixture to a boil.

Reduce to a simmer and cook for 5 minutes.

Stir in the noodles and cook for a few more minutes.

Serve immediately and enjoy!

Sriracha Zucchini Soup

Zoodles, chicken, and sriracha join forces and create this powerful recipe that will knock your flu out in a second. Add some lime zest for a zestier taste.

Serves: 2

Ready In: 15 minutes

Ingredients:

- 2 cups Zucchini Noodles
- 8 ounces Chicken Breast, chopped
- 4 cups Chicken Broth
- ½ tbsp. Lime Juice
- 2 tsp Sriracha
- ½ tsp minced Garlic
- 1 tsp Soy Sauce
- 2 tsp chopped Cilantro
- 1 Spring Onion, sliced

Preparation:

Combine the broth, ginger, and garlic, in a pot.

Bring it to a boil and add the chicken.

Cook for about 10 minutes.

Add zoodles and lime juice, and cook for about 3 minutes.

Stir in the sriracha.

Serve immediately topped with cilantro.

Enjoy!

Chinese Seaweed and Pork Soup

Simple to make, healthy, and super nourishing, this bowl of Chinese soup with seafood, tofu, and yummy pork, will warm you up and satisfy all your senses.

Serves: 5

Ready In: 25 minutes

Ingredients:

- 1 Organic Stock Cube
- ½ pound ground Pork
- 5 cups Water
- ½ sheet Chinese Dried Seaweed
- 1 block of Silken Tofu, cubed

Marinade:

- ¼ tsp Salt
- ¼ tsp Pepper
- 1 ½ tsp Cornstarch
- ¾ tbsp. Soy Sauce
- 1 tsp Garlic Oil

Preparation:

Combine the pork with the marinade ingredients.

Shape the mixture into balls. Set aside.

Place the water in a large pot and bring it to a boil.

Add the stock cube.

When dissolved drop the pork meatballs into the soup.

Cook for about 5 minutes.

Add tofu and seaweed and cook for 1 minute.

Serve immediately and enjoy!

Japanese Rice Soup

Originally called Zosui, this recipe is a Japanese rice soup that is a version of congee. Rice cooked with veggies and eggs in a tummy-warming stock that will be your best friend during those cold winter months.

Serves: 2

Ready In: 15 minutes

Ingredients:

- 2 tsp Soy Sauce
- 2 Eggs, beaten
- 17 ounces Dashi Stock
- 7 ounces Cooked Rice
- 3 Shitake Mushrooms, sliced
- 1 large Carrot, grated
- A pinch of Salt

Preparation:

Combine the stock, salt, and soy sauce, in a pot over medium heat.

Bring it to a boil.

Add the mushrooms and carrot and cook for a few minutes, until tender.

Stir in the rice and drizzle the eggs over while stirring in a circular motion to make egg ribbons.

Cook for about 20 seconds.

Serve immediately with chopped shallots.

Enjoy!

Korean Soybean Soup

Fermented soybean paste, oyster mushrooms, zucchini, and tofu are cooked together in a nourishing Korean stock for a delicious and authentic Korean soup that will please absolutely everyone.

Serves: 3

Ready In: 25 minutes

Ingredients

- 2 Green Onions, sliced
- 6 ounces Zucchini, sliced
- 8 ounces Tofu, cubed
- 3 ½ tbsp. Korean Fermented Soybean Paste
- 4 ounces Oyster Mushrooms, sliced
- 2 ½ cups Korean Stock
- 1 Chili, sliced, optional

Preparation:

Pour the stock in a pot.

Whisk in the soybean paste to avoid any lumps.

Stir in the mushroom, zucchini, and tofu, and bring the soup to a boil.

Cook for 3 minutes and stir in the chili and green onion.

Serve immediately and enjoy!

Kabocha Squash Soup

Golden, delicious, and absolutely luscious, this miso infused kabocha squash soup has the power to nourish even after the first sip. Serve topped with crunchy toasted walnuts or croutons.

Serves: 4

Ready In: 30 minutes

Ingredients:

- 2 tbsp. Oil
- 3 cups Water
- 6 cups diced Kabocha Squash
- 1 Onion, diced
- 3 Garlic Cloves minced
- 2 tbsp. White Miso Paste
- 1 ½ tbsp. grated Ginger

Preparation:

Heat the oil in a large pot.

Add onion and squash and cook for about 10 minutes.

Stir in the ginger and garlic and cook for an additional minute.

Add water and bring the mixture to a boil.

Reduce to simmer and cook for 10 minutes.

Blend the soup with a hand blender.

In some hot water, dissolve the miso and stir it into the soup.

Cook for about 1 more minute.

Serve and enjoy!

Instant Short Rib Soup

A classic Korean rib soup, originally called Galbitang, is prepared in the instant pot for a much more easy and convenient lunch. Beef short ribs and Korean radish play the main role in this recipe.

Serves: 6-8

Ready In: 35 minutes

Ingredients:

- 1 ½ pound Beef Ribs
- 8 cups Water
- 4 Green Onions, sliced
- 1 Yellow Onion
- 2 tbsp. chopped Garlic
- ½ Korean Radish, cut into chunks
- 2 slices of Ginger
- 2 tsp Soy Sauce
- 1 tsp Sea Salt

Preparation:

Place all of the ingredients in your Instant Pot.

Choose the SOUP function and cook for 30 minutes.

Release the pressure naturally.

Serve and enjoy!

Coconut and Lentil Soup

Golden in color and irresistible in taste, this coconut and lentil soup is a real crowd pleaser. Serve topped with a spoonful of cooked white rice for an even more filling lunch.

Serves: 4

Ready In: 40 minutes

Ingredients:

- ½ pound Lentils
- 4 cups Water
- 1 tbsp. Oil
- 2 Carrots, diced
- 1 inch Ginger, grated
- 2 Garlic Cloves, minced
- 1 Onion, diced
- 14 ounces Coconut Milk
- ½ tbsp. Turmeric
- Salt, to taste

Preparation:

Heat the oil in a large pot.

Add onions and cook for 3 minutes.

Add garlic, and ginger and cook for one more minute.

Stir in turmeric and carrots and cook for one more minute.

Add lentils and water.

Bring the soup to a boil and cook on low for 20 minutes.

Stir in the coconut milk and season with salt.

Blend if you want it to be creamy.

Serve and enjoy!

Mason Jar Pho Soup

This pho soup from a mason jar is the ultimate nourishing lunch that you can bring with you to your office. Vegetables and rice noodles give this pho a delicate, filling, and flavorful taste.

Serves: 1

Ready In: 20 minutes

Ingredients:

- 2 tbsp. Soy Sauce
- 1 tsp minced Garlic
- ½ cup sliced Carrots
- 1 tsp minced Ginger
- 1 cup cooked Rice Noodles
- ½ cup julienned Red Pepper
- ¼ cup chopped Green Onion
- 3 cups Chicken Stock

Preparation:

In a pot add the chicken stock and bring it to a boil over medium heat.

Add the remaining ingredients in a jar.

Pour the boiling stock over.

Let the soup sit for 15 minutes before consuming.

Serve and enjoy!

Thai Soup with Pumpkin and Coconut

Flavorful, delicious, and incredibly comforting, this creamy pumpkin and coconut milk Thai soup is a real keeper. The curry paste gives this soup a powerful kick and make it even more delightful.

Serves: 4

Ready In: 60 minutes

Ingredients:

- 2 ½ cups Chicken Stock   600 ml
- 1 tbsp. Oil
- 2 Garlic Cloves, crushed
- 4 ounces Baby Potatoes, chopped   110 gm
- 1 Onion, chopped
- 2 ½ pounds Pumpkin, chopped   1 Kg
- ¼ cup Thai Red Curry Paste
- 14 ounces Coconut Milk   400 ml
- 2 tbsp. chopped Coriander
- 2 tbsp. chopped Peanuts

Preparation

Heat the oil in a pot.

Add onion and cook for 4 minutes.

Add potato and pumpkin chunks and cook for another 5 minutes.

Add garlic and cook for one minute.

Stir in the curry paste and cook it for 2 minutes.

Pour the stock over and stir to combine. Bring to a boil.

Reduce to a simmer and cook for 35 minutes.

Blend the soup using a hand blender.

Stir in the coconut milk and cook for 5 more minutes.

Serve topped with coriander and peanuts.

Enjoy!

Gingery and Garlicky Turmeric and Tofu Soup

Looking for something nourishing and anti-inflammatory to kick the annoying cold? Then what better way to do so than with a bowl of this comforting, soothing, but super delicious soup?

Serves: 2

Ready In: 25 minutes

Ingredients:

- ½ tsp Pepper
- 1 tsp Oil
- 7 Garlic Cloves, minced
- 7 ounces Tofu, cubed
- 1 ½ inch Ginger, grated
- 2 tsp Soy Sauce
- 1 tsp Apple Cider Vinegar
- 1 tbsp. White Mellow Miso
- ½ Chili, deseeded and sliced
- ½ Red Bell Pepper, sliced
- 3 cups Water
- 1 tsp Turmeric
- 1 tsp Maple Syrup
- ½ cup shredded Carrots

Preparation:

Heat the oil in a pot.

Add chili, garlic, and ginger, and cook for a few minutes.

Stir in the pepper and carrots and cook for 4 minutes.

Stir in water, tofu, soy sauce, turmeric, and maple.

Bring the mixture to a boil.

Simmer for 4 minutes.

Whisk in the remaining ingredients and cook for 3 more minutes.

Serve and enjoy!

Vietnamese Sour Fish Soup

Rich in amazing flavor contrasts, this sour Vietnamese soup with fish, okra, tomato, and bean sprouts, has a delightful texture that is at the same time crunchy and spongy. Amazing lunch choice!

Serves: 4

Ready In: 15 minutes

Ingredients:

- 1 tbsp. Oil
- 1 ½ tbsp. Fish Sauce
- ¼ cup Tamari
- 1 cup Fish Chunks
- 10 Okra, cut into pieces
- 5 ½ cups Water
- 1 ½ tsp Sugar
- 1 ½ tsp Salt
- 1 Onion, sliced
- ½ pound Tomatoes, chopped1 tsp Cumin
- 2 cups Bean Sprouts

Preparation:

Heat the oil in a pot over medium heat.

Add the onion and cook for a few minutes.

Stir in water, tamari, sugar, salt, and fish sauce. Bring the mixture to a boil.

Reduce to simmer and cook for 5 minutes.

Stir in okra and cook for 2 minutes.

Add the remaining ingredients and cook for another 30 seconds.

Serve immediately and enjoy!

Conclusion

Now that you have 40 soothing, nourishing, and deeply pleasing Asian soup recipes, it is time to start cooking and fill your kitchen with the irresistible Asian flavors that will draw everyone to the dining table.

Did you find these recipes tasty? Leave a review and let others know. Your feedback will be greatly appreciated.

Thank you and happy cooking!

Author's Afterthoughts

Thanks ever so much to each of my cherished readers for investing the time to read this book!

I know you could have picked from many other books but you chose this one. So a big thanks for downloading this book and reading all the way to the end.

If you enjoyed this book or received value from it, I'd like to ask you for a favor. Please take a few minutes to post an honest and heartfelt review on Amazon.com. Your support does make a difference and helps to benefit other people.

Thanks!

Daniel Humphreys

About the Author

Daniel Humphreys

Many people will ask me if I am German or Norman, and my answer is that I am 100% unique! Joking aside, I owe my cooking influence mainly to my mother who was British! I can certainly make a mean Sheppard's pie, but when it comes to preparing Bratwurst sausages and drinking beer with friends, I am also all in!

I am taking you on this culinary journey with me and hope you can appreciate my diversified background. In my 15 years career as a chef, I never had a dish returned to me by one of clients, so that should say something about me! Actually, I will take that back. My worst critic is my four years old son, who refuses to taste anything that is green color. That shall pass, I am sure.

My hope is to help my children discover the joy of cooking and sharing their creations with their loved ones, like I did all my life. When you develop a passion for cooking and my suspicious is that you have one as well, it usually sticks for life. The best advice I can give anyone as a professional chef is invest. Invest your time, your heart in each meal you are creating. Invest also a little money in good cooking hardware and quality ingredients. But most of all enjoy every meal you prepare with YOUR friends and family!